Contents

Acknowledgement

Introduction

Dear Friend,

Today is the beginning of a new day.

Helping you find the path to your dream is our priority.

Let the journey begin.

Please read and feedback your thoughts.

Thank you.

Alex Gordon

alex.whatisyourdream@gmail.com

This book is published by

Dream Success Ltd
5 Blackhorse Lane
Walthamstow
London E17 6DS

www.alex-gordon.net

First published in Great Britain in 2012.

The right of Alex Gordon to be identified as the author of this work has been asserted by him in accordance with the Copyright, Designs and Patents act 1988.

ISBN: 978-1-62050-105-4

British Library Cataloguing-in-Publication data
A catalogue record of this book is available from the British library

Library of Congress Cataloguing-in-Publication Data
A catalogue record of this book is available from the Library of Congress

Cover concept, design by Kinga White
Typeset, PALS Secretarial Services

Acknowledgements

It is a pleasure to know I can
share my thoughts with you.
Thank you.
Alex Gordon

Thanks to my mum and dad Miriam and Lester, for not giving up on me. Throughout all the trials of growing a young family, they did their best to instil Godly values.

Thanks to my wife Sharon, soul mate of over twenty-five years of marriage, putting up with all the quirks. Encouraging me at all times to share my thoughts, and being there even when I am not around, travelling to conferences and seminars.

Thanks to my beautiful children, Jasinta 24, Jarome 20 and Jaidon 11. Each with their own unique gifting, ability and talent; having the confidence to pursue their individual dreams.

Thanks for being great kids.

Thanks to the men that I have had the benefit of working with over the years, the ones that gave life to Life Builders UK. Thanks to the young men and boys who participated in our programmes such as "Boyz 2 Men Summer Camp".

Note from the Author

What If,

What if you had done all the things you wanted to do to date, what difference would it have made?

What if you had listened to your parents and done everything they asked you to, would life have been different?

What if you had been the perfect student or the perfect child growing up, would life have been different?

What if you had been the perfect employee and done all the chores without moaning, would you have got the promotion?

What if you had said yes to that handsome gentleman, or that rogue of a boyfriend, would life have been different?

What if you could live your life again, would it be any different?

We often spend time looking back with regret but the only thing you can change is ahead of you, the FUTURE.
If only you had been a good child, a better student, a better wife, a better husband, a better employee, a better businessman, a better politician, past your degree, said yes. What would have happened?

The past is behind you, focus ahead and change the future. That is your greatest power.

Introduction

At last, I have managed to buckle down and write what I have been speaking about for the last ten years, encouraging and teaching on.

Call me a dreamer or whatever you like, I have had this project on hold for such a long time that my closest friends are becoming restless, waiting for this book "What is your dream?"

Over many years I realised that all that I had learnt at school was not relevant to the life I was leading. Endless hours learning and absorbing information to then totally disregard in later years.

No one ever took the time to find out what I was dreaming about, and engage in my little world.

It is no surprise that all I talk about now is dreams and aspirations, encouraging people to follow the desires of their heart and not waiting for some outer space experience to provide meaning and purpose to their lives.

So, I hope you can glean something from the words that follow, giving hope, inspiration, building trust and confidence in your Gifts, Abilities and Talents.

1 The Big World of Dreamers

*Dream lofty dreams, and as you dream, so shall you become.
Your vision is the promise of what you shall one day be.
(James Allen)*

The World of Big Dreamers consists of men and women who recognise their calling in life and pursue that path with all their soul and mind. Big Dreamers are visionaries that have done and are doing the Vision Walk against all the obstacles that life throws at them.

Do not confuse these visionaries with daydreamers (people who dream but take no action to fulfil what they see). The heart of the matter is, connecting with that inner power that is giving you direction.

A very rich man by the name of Jacob had twelve sons one of which he favoured more than the others. There was something about this son that he couldn't put his finger on; he was very different from his brothers. His name was Joseph. At 17 Joseph had a dream that he shared with his brothers. To his surprise they were not happy for him, instead they plotted against him.

> As a dreamer who tries to connect with what he sees, the public do not always understand what you are saying at the time. There is often a very long time gap for others to catch the vision.

Martin Luther King Jr., stood on the steps of the Lincoln Memorial Washington 1963 in front of more than 200,000 people and addressed an agitated crowd, an audience seeking more for their lives, fed up with inequalities, segregation and the injustices they were experiencing and being treated as second class citizens not worthy.

"What is your dream?" as he stared into the eyes of a forgotten people that were being encouraged to stand up and fight with their words and non-violent action.

"What is your dream?" as he tried to ignite the fire, the passion for life in their bellies.

"What is your dream?" as he bore the weight of the struggle felt by his people, and even those who died during the struggle. They too were crying out from their graves.

His message transcends time, discrimination and racial disharmony. Simply, he dreamt of a world where men, women, boys and girls would be equal, treated equal so they felt equal. Equal in all opportunities, equal access to all available resources.

Some forty years later we are still battling

Some forty years later we are still battling with the same issues of passing judgement on each other. Years after his death we look back and appreciate what he was saying and somehow idolise him but at the time he was speaking, we were prepared to shut him up.

Although his life was brought to an abrupt end in 1963, his words live on, his dream lives on, his words of hope are still challenging the society in which we live, and we are proud of him.

For the short time we are alive I hope we learn to appreciate the differences in each other and recognise that the voice we each carry serves a purpose, even though it may not be evident at the time.

Do not hide what you have, discover it and live it – **What is your dream?**

The Successful companies of the next decade will be the ones that use the digital tools to reinvent the way they work. These companies will make decisions quickly, act efficiently, and directly touch their customers in positive ways. (Bill Gates)

Bill Gates is one of those entrepreneurs who had his eyes on a different world. One he probably dreamt about and created through his own eyes before anyone would get on board. He saw the digital era in a way that most of us failed to acknowledge. He was like Moses leading the people into the promised land of a personal computer on every desk across the world.

How is the technology affecting you?

Bills Gates and Steve Jobs' contribution to the digital era has created a generation of winners, those who understand and command the development of the Software industry. Creating a generation of new wealth from software. The industry has now given small businessmen the ability to trade like a big company being located anywhere in the world but connected to what is happening.

Richard Branson founded his whole career on the most phenomenal PR known to man

Richard Branson, an unorthodox businessman understood the power of the media in building his brand, Virgin. He was known for taking trips in his balloon around the world in the blaze of publicity, most of which was free. He bought an Island over 20 years ago, what was he thinking? He saw an opportunity and he took it. Today celebrities pay close to $250k per week to hire his island. What did he see that you and I never? How did we miss it?

Are there any opportunities left?

Opportunities are available to everyone regardless of background or race. The key is you must be looking.

Ever bought a car and after you take delivery, everywhere you look you can see a car like yours; almost as if everyone has deliberately bought your type of car.

Opportunities work in the same way. Commit to looking for an opportunity and expect it from a variety of sources. At some point just like the car it will be everywhere. This is called the Reticular Activation System. The RAS in your brain brings to your attention all relevant information.

Your reticular activating system is like a filter between your conscious mind and your subconscious mind. It takes instructions from your conscious mind and passes them on to your subconscious.

A Car

Henry Ford dreamt of a car that had one colour, black. He built no other car in his lifetime. But the fact remains he built a car. Without his dream and later a vision that was made reality we would not have seen his car.

> **Whether you think you can or whether you think you can't, you're right!**
> **(Henry Ford)**

Whatsoever you think your dream to be it is so. The anointing or the energy comes from you and your belief.

Dyke and Dryden in Cosmetics

At long last Britain is beginning to produce homegrown entrepreneurs among its ethnic population. But they will remain few and far between without more government and business support. By Anna Foster **(How They Made A Million)**

First Black Cosmetic Entrepreneurs in the UK

Dyke and Dryden Ltd, one of Britain's most successful black hair products business, was the first to identify the market for Afro-Caribbean products of hair and skin care. They suffered much prejudice in the early days from the established institutions for funding and expansion. However, this did not stop them.

The directors Len Dyke, Dudley Dryden and Tony Wade were visionary pioneers in the black community paving the way for the development of the multi-million black cosmetic industry in the UK.

There are some people who never saw success from a distance but persevered with what they loved doing until it became successful. Others became successful despite the obstacles that were in their path even though there were times when they had pressed the self-destruct button.

Do you deserve Success?

In the book called 'No more tears' the author Sotonye Diri interviewed several successful businessmen and women from the Afro-Caribbean community who described their path to success. I would like us to look at Ade Shokoya, Alexander Amosu, Dionne Jude and Levi Roots.

Ade Shokoya

"If I wanted to be successful I had to change my social circle."

This young man was not someone who had mapped out a career path to succeed. Whilst being involved in gangs for over ten years, he survived two prison sentences and managed to obtain a first class degree in Information Systems. He attempted to study only on the encouragement of a young female student who saw him hanging around the college every day. He later built two successful companies.

> The proven path to success is not one-dimensional, there are many paths but there seems to be one prevailing key, to become successful, you must WORK at it.

Alexander Amosu

He made his first million at the age of twenty-four.

Alexander showed an entrepreneurial instinct from an early age. He started with a newspaper round and felt the power of making money. Whilst studying for his GCSE's he ran a hire company for sound systems and promoted thirty-seven parties per night.

While at University something happened that changed his life forever. He created a ring tone in his bedroom that catapulted him into the student market for mobile phone ring tones. He launched RnB Ring Tones and made £1.6million in his first year.

Dionne Jude

This young lady loved the dancehall scene, a type of dance originating out of the island of Jamaica. She created her own clothes line to fit her outrageous look. After post graduate studies at University she became a careers adviser but her dream idea, Nappy Cakes UK, a baby's gift basket of nappies and other useful items surpassed all expectations when Selfridges decided to sell the first gift basket.

Who has the blueprint to success?

Is there a certain path that you must take to be successful? Must you be of a certain colour or race to succeed? Do we all have an idea that could make us successful?

Levi Roots

An annual season ticket holder of Notting Hill carnival, year on year selling jerk chicken with his favourite sauce. Levi Roots knew how to cook West Indian food and practiced the craft for over twenty-five years.

Does your idea depend on the business plan or you the dreamer?

In 2008 with no big business experience he was invited on to the Dragon's Den, a programme for entrepreneurs seeking finance where they are interviewed by successful businessmen and women.

Levi Roots sang his proposal for the millionaire businessmen and women. This was very unorthodox as he had no business plan and did not understand the numbers.

They loved his unique style and bought into the idea. What did they see? Was it the unproven sauce or was it the dreamer standing there with his guitar and dreadlocks? Today Sainsbury's, Tesco and Subway stock his Reggae Reggae sauce. His product lines have extended from the sauce to cookbooks and a restaurant. He is now worth over £30million.

Can you cook West Indian food? Could that have been you?

What is stopping you sharing your culinary skills?

What is the common denominator to all these stories?

Success does not appear to depend on the amount of knowledge you acquire nor as we used to believe, dependent upon the University education you received. It is very much linked to serving the community at large.

Creating a product that you enjoy making and finding thousands of

You can be a dreamer and a doer too, if you remove one word from your vocabulary impossible. (Dr Robert Schuller)

Not everyone is going to share your dream, vision or great idea. While some may think it is possible and give you all the encouragement you need, others will put themselves in your shoes and because they cannot see themselves doing it, they think it is **IMPOSSIBLE**.

Do you see the possibilities that exist around your life?

In fact there are three kinds of people that will influence the way you think, two of them you must avoid at all cost.

- Dream Breakers
- Dream Blockers
- Dream Builders

Dream Breakers

These people have no dream or vision of life of their own, their sole purpose in life is to discourage the unknown, the untested and the unfamiliar and kill your joy. Unable to accept and receive your excitement but at every opportunity throwing water on your fire with their words of doubt and discouragement.

"Can you really do that"?
"Others have failed at that"
"Why are you wasting your time"?
"Stick to your job"
"You are not bright enough"

What kind of words has been spoken to you that has deterred you moving forward?

How did you feel at the time?

Dream Blockers

Blockers are any person, situation or event that accentuates the feeling of fear or doubt, presenting barriers or obstacles that seem insurmountable. Forcing you to stay in your comfort zone and not venture beyond that point.

In Karate Kid 1 Mr Meyagi was coaching the young man Daniel to overcome the thresholds of;

- **Pain**
  Feeling the pain but convincing his mind that it can be done so he was able to break the pieces of wood after being shown how.

- **Almost giving up**
  Even when you feel you have given everything you think you have, pushing that extra mile. Our body has reserves that our conscious mind does not immediately recognise. There were times when Daniel felt he could not do it. Could not concentrate, could not get the moves right.

- **Internal Procrastination**
  Mr Meyagi encouraged Daniel to keep practising, as action is the enemy of procrastination. How many times have you left something until tomorrow, "not feeling it right now", feeling tired after work or cannot wake on time. Only action that is taken today will prevent procrastination.

- **Negative thinking**
  The automatic negative thoughts that we have every day will only subside with your belief and confessions. I can do this. Daniel talked himself into practising even when he was washing the car.

Dream Builders

These are co-dreamers who delight in seeing people grow, develop and take action. They encourage, support, push and take a keen interest in what you are doing. These are the men and women who watch your back at all times. They are what you would call self-appointed mentors.

- Motivating you
- Encouraging you
- Navigating you
- Trusting you
- Casting your ongoing development
- Reality check

Motivation

Every person requires food to give energy to the body. That is what motivation does for the spirit. It propels you into action and provides sustenance even when you feel weak.

Encouragement and excitement

Maintaining your level of excitement in any new venture requires constant encouragement from those who care about you most. Someone has to be watching your corner. In the boxing ring there is always someone in the corner shouting you on and they are prepared to act on your behalf when the moment requires it.

Navigation

Directions are very important in any journey. Every person needs help at some point to navigate the way. Even though I have had a number of disagreements with my wife while driving, about the route we took; the Sat Nav has probably saved my marriage. I make sure the voice is the one I enjoy listening to.

Trust

There will be moments in your life when you need to rely on someone else to carry out a task or represent you in some capacity. This will only be possible if there is trust. Trust is built on relationship. This relationship can either be a contractual one like that of an employee performing all the tasks within the scope of a job description, or one built on friendship.

Ongoing development

Despite many years of education and training, it is not possible to know everything there is about your industry. The digital era has not stopped developing in the last twenty years. The technology has advanced so quickly that we need to keep abreast of the benefits to your industry or area of work.

Reality check

It is very easy to get carried away and caught up with a project or idea. Utilising all your resources to keep it alive when it should have closed. What works or is not working must always be assessed to take corrective action.

Your Ideal Picture

> All successful people, men and women who are big dreamers, they imagine that the future could be ideal in every respect and they work every day toward their distant vision, that goal or purpose. (Brian Tracey)

You must paint a picture of what the ideal looks like whether it's a business, a lifestyle or a project. It is smart to work towards what you can see, a picture that you are painting for your life. Be very careful who you allow to paint on your canvass because it will affect your ability to see your picture.

Six keys to identifying a Dreamer:

1. **V**alue thoughts and ideas
   A thinker, a seer, acting on thoughts and ideas and able to paint a mental picture of the ideal future.

2. **I**nnovative
   Able to discover alternative ways of getting the results required.

3. **S**elective
   Driven by what they see and very selective about who they work with.

4. **I**nspiring
   Their lives inspire others and are a testament to what can be accomplished.

5. **O**ngoing development
   Learning and adopting to new things immediately, whatever it takes to keep moving.

6. **N**ever giving up

Self propelled, having the energy to keep on keeping on.

My Action Points

1. Identify people who have impacted your life and explain how.

2. Identify how you would like to impact the lives of other people.

3. Identify obstacles that you have encountered.

4.   What strategies are you applying to overcome your obstacles?

5.   If you were given the role of President or Prime Minister, what would you do?

6.   If you were given £1,500,000 pounds as in Brewster's Millions and you could not spend it on yourself or family, what would you do with it?

2 What Do You Want For Your Life?

*If you want to have more, you must first have
to become more.   (Jim Rohn)*

If you ask nine year olds what they want, they are able to reel off a shopping list of all the things recorded in their brain as though they were waiting for this one moment just to be asked the question.

"What do you want?"

It is not enough to want a game, a child can tell you the type of game, what it does, the cost and where you can buy it, specifics.

Adulthood takes away the fun out of dreaming

Ask an adult the same question and after much deliberation probably ten to fifteen minutes' delay, they would still be unsure as to what they really want for their life. A child is not bothered whether it is realistic or not or even affordable.

Adulthood takes away the fun of just dreaming fearless innocent thoughts about what life could be like.

Ten years ago I used to get up every day and go to work just to pay the bills, working for the money. I was in the city of London earning very good money but my heart had left the job.

Dreamt about running my own business

I dreamt about running my own business, I even had business cards printed with the name of my consultancy sitting on my crummy little desk in my home office.

One thing I enjoyed doing and looked forward to on a Monday morning was encouraging the staff and enquiring about their weekends. You can just imagine on a Monday so many people not wanting to be at work.

People going to jobs they hate

According to Les Brown the motivational speaker, 'heart attacks is at it's highest on a Monday morning'. People going to jobs they hate.

One Monday morning I arrived at work in a very foul mood, I did not want to be there. I sat at my desk and did not speak to anyone. One member of staff sensing the mood I was in, approached me and said, "Is everything okay?" "You normally give such great encouragement on a Monday morning, but today you are so quiet, is there anything we can do?"

I knew it! I felt it! There was more to my life than what I was being paid to do. A few weeks later a senior manager said, "Alex, you remind me of that motivational guy, Anthony Robbins, do you know him?"

This was just another confirmation for me that it was time. Time for a change, a new beginning. I relayed these events to my mentor, the desire to do something else, to run my own business and the two separate incidents took place.

Be careful of what you ask for, it might just happen

He said, "Alex, be careful of what you ask for, it might just happen".

Two months later on a Monday, while sitting at my desk and looking busy, the Finance Director summoned me to the boardroom. "What did he want?" My heart was pounding, my head in turmoil.

You're Fired

The month end had passed, reports had been distributed and there were no scheduled meetings in the diary, "What could he want?"

As my heart raced, more like missed a beat; I went to the boardroom where I was greeted with pleasantries.

"Alex, sit down", the pounding in my head got louder. "Glad you could join us, how are things?" I thought just get on with it man. "We are making you redundant, there is no more work. I knew he never liked me, could that be why I was the chosen one. But I remembered ……….

This was the moment I had been preparing and waiting for, "Eureka". "You're fired", no, "I am free". Ten seconds later my head said, "What are you going to tell your family?" How are the bills going to be paid?"

I left the office that day and never looked back

That was nearly ten years ago. I left the office that day and never looked back. The good book says that God grants you the desire of your heart. But who would have guessed that this would happen so quickly.

Does that sound familiar to you? Are you in a similar situation, wanting more for your life? Well, where did this all begin?

What was the sequence of events that led to the termination of my contract and to the beginning of a new life?

It began with a desire for something more for my life. A frantic scream in my spirit, my soul.

A sense of discontentment had consumed my heart, an inner voice was pushing me to stretch myself, move beyond the boundaries I had surrounded myself with.

What Do You Want for Your Life?

Yes, that secure job was the boundary I felt I could not go beyond; because of the lifestyle it afforded me. Regular reliable stable income could have stayed thirty-eight years.

Like a car stuck in the snow and no matter how hard you accelerate, you are unable to move in the direction you want to because you are stuck. There is no grit on the ice to give the car grip on the surface.

For a long time I felt someone or something had been speaking to me, I was in a strange place wanting a change but too scared to take the plunge.

Have you have ever heard the story of the crabs in a barrel. Every time a crab starts to climb out of the barrel the others pull him back down, they grab his back, his heels or claw him back. Has life ever done that to you, you take one step only to feel stuck, threatened and inadequate or talk yourself out of taking action today?

There is always tomorrow. The challenge is, tomorrow is never now. The more you delay the more tomorrow looks better until a week goes by, then a month and before you know it a year has gone by and still no action.

The Great Discovery

It is not what you are born with or where you are born that

makes you what you become. It is what you do with what you have, how you develop that helps you to become the man or woman that you are becoming.

What do you want for your life?

I had remained motionless or inactive for too long, not really living but enduring a situation. Being satisfied with my lot while my heart was yearning for a life of its own.

I learned some valuable lessons that day.

Valuable Lessons

- Listen to your heart
- Do not ignore your gut feeling of discomfort and uneasiness
- Take action
- Feel the fear and act anyway
- Champion your own cause

Listen to Your Heart

When you feel strongly about something, and no matter how hard you try to ignore or block it out, it stands there staring you in the face, just like a person, talking to you and questioning your inactivity. At that precise moment you rationalise your thoughts and drown your feelings as though they were noise. It pays to listen, it is cheaper, the mistakes or detours we sometimes take could easily have been avoided. I realise it now.

Do Not Ignore Your Gut Feeling of Discomfort and Uneasiness

Feeling restless and discontent with a situation is like our internal temperature gauge. Keeping track of how we feel, are we at boiling point and unable to take any more?

Do not ignore your inner voice, your conscience, follow through. The level of dissatisfaction and uneasiness is the calibration on a thermometer.

Are you going to actually wait until boiling point to act? This may be the point of no return where you say or do something you later regret and cannot reverse.

Take Action

Imagine you are standing in the middle of a motorway with cars approaching on all sides, what do you do? Stand still and scream for help or step in front of the moving cars. Whatever you decide to do, make a decision to act or else you will eventually get run over.

Have you ever stood at a pedestrian crossing waiting for the lollipop lady to help you cross while she is chatting to someone, forgetting you are there, totally preoccupied, not doing her job? Is that you? Busy doing the wrong thing at the wrong time.

Following your heart is about following up in small steps or even discussing what you are thinking with a like-minded traveller. This will get you to the point where you are doing the right thing at the right time. No one can show you the right time.

Feel the Fear and Act Anyway

Probably the hardest thing for anyone to do, is moving beyond that point in your life where it feels like life or death, and convincing yourself that you are going to be okay.

My wife is frightened of heights and every time we cross on a bridge or hover any distance above the ground she becomes very tense and you can see the fear building. This is what happens to most of us. We become emotionally crippled by our fears.

Championing Your Cause

Have you ever been so busy doing things for other people just to forget what is happening to you? It does make you feel better for a short time but the fact remains, nothing has changed in your situation and will not change until you take the necessary action. So championing you as a cause will help you. Give the project a name "Operation Get Me Out of Here" and recruit your friends and family for a few hours for positive input and action.

Make A Dream List

If you don't know where you are going, you might wind up somewhere else. (Yogi Berra)

I have heard this so many times. But it is not what you hear that changes your life; it is what you do with what you hear. Every conference I have ever attended, even at church, at the beginning of the year you are instructed to make a list. When you hear it you say "Yeh, Yeh I've got a list in my head". But things only come to life when you actually sit down and start to ink all the things you would really like to do. They do not have to make sense just write them down.

How do you get your thoughts flowing?

Think and then jot down what you thought on, it's your aim:

1. What do you enjoy doing
2. What do you like looking at
3. Where do you like visiting
4. Think of your ideal house, car or holiday
5. Who do you like having around you

Getting lost in London is not very hard but ignoring your SATNAV is foolhardy. This list will help you get focused on where you are going. At least you can tell your friends where you want to go.

**The indispensable first step to getting the things you want
out of life is this: decide what you want. (Ben Stein)**

Do not wait for things to happen to you as though you are a boat without a sail and no engine to drive you. Make a decision today that will change the course of your life and the life of others you connect with. Jim Rohn said, "You cannot change the direction of the wind but you can change your sail".

Some Decisions are Difficult to Make

Decisions are sometimes difficult to make and therefore requires wise counsel, able men and women who can inform and coach you but not decide for you.

There is a story of a man sitting by a pool for a long time, wanting to go in but unable to stir himself to take the plunge, unable to move because he was crippled. At certain times of the day it was said the pool had healing qualities. Now if that were you, would you not ask someone for help just to get in? Could it be your moment that you need to dive into the pool? He never asked for help, he just sat there, waiting. Could he have rolled himself in?

Imagine the pool for a moment; what possible actions could the crippled man have taken to get into the pool?

What would you have done?
Make a few notes

At times you feel as though this is it, there is no way out, no options, no alternative. Creating the biggest pity party for yourself does not change the situation; you might like all the attention from everyone, feeling sorry for you. But that is not the intended outcome. You may be unable to see clearly right now. In a few moments, days or years it will be clearer but don't wait thirty-eight years doing nothing like someone you know.

Take small steps but frequently towards your intended outcome.
Make a list of possible actions that you could take to change your situation giving a reason why.

Possible Actions	Why

Stepping Out of 9 to 5

The nine to five paradigm has served us for probably generations since the war, providing an obedient workforce that turn up every day and do their part in exchange for a set pay. Anyone who does not fit into this mould was seen as a deviant or a maverick, not capable of settling down to a normal life.

Over the years we have developed flexible working hours, part-time workers and contract workers to cater for a more diverse workforce who want more out of life than just work. Work needs to fit in where we want the balance most.

Work life balance is a concept that has grown over the years and more people are demanding an alternative to the way they currently work.

Let us look at what Robert Kiyosaki first called the four quadrants in his book Rich Dad Poor Dad;

E	**B**
PPP **(Position Payment Plan)**	BPP **(Business Profit Plan)**
S	**I**
SPP **(Self Payment Plan)**	MM **(Money Mastery)**

- Position Payment Plan – Employee
- Self Payment Plan – Self Employed
- Business Profit Plan - Business Systems
- MM – Money Mastery – Investor

Position Payment Plan (PPP)

The Position Payment Plan (PPP) is the one that employees are plugged into. No matter how good you are at your job you are paid for the position you hold within the organisation, the agreed sum every month.

Everyone operates within the defined scope of a job description and no more. At the end of the year you might be considered for a pay rise, it is not guaranteed. If you are fortunate enough to work in the more senior positions then you will have a benefits package.

Self-Payment Plan (SPP)

The Self Payment Plan (SPP) is those people who decide to take a plunge into business and work for themselves. Sacking their boss and determining their pay all by themselves. The whole business depends on their activity and no one works as hard as or better than they do.

Another term to describe this person is a Solopreneur. Many work at home businesses operate on this basis. With the advancements in technology they are able to communicate and operate like a much larger profiled business without the associated overheads.

Business Payment Plan (BPP)

The Business Payment Plan (BPP) is one built around a business system that operates wherever you may be and does not depend solely on your efforts.

The system responds to the input of a number of other people and is able to generate profits independently of the owners. According to Jim Rohn profit is better than wages.

Money Mastery (MM)

Money Mastery (MM) is a system where money works for you. Your investments produce returns that meet your pre-determined profile or investment criteria.

Imagine buying 1,000 shares of Microsoft at say $5 dollar a share thirty years ago, how much would they be worth today? The spread of your investments minimises the risk among stable long term and high growth products.

Another aspect of this is the **Money Matrix** where a product is distributed in high volumes with a low price, or at a low volume with a very high ticket price. In both cases a product requires a distribution network to make it work. Take a look at Amazon the book sellers or the large supermarket chains. How will you price your product?

Where Are You Now?

Review the quadrant and decide where you are. Are you unhappy in your paid employment and would like to start a business part-time? Where would you rather be?
What difference would it make to your life?

There is a process that you must consider when making a change that affects every aspect of your life.

Which Way?

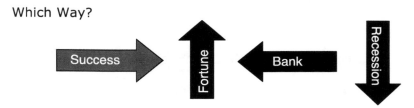

Stepping Out

To move from the left to the right side or from top left to bottom left requires a paradigm shift in your thinking and behaviour not only to consider what is demanded of you but also to take the necessary steps. This Stepping Out point is beyond your comfort zone, or the box in which you have been operating for so long.

Practice stepping out of your box

Draw a box on the floor large enough so you can stand in it. Step inside the box, think about everything you have done to date, how it made you feel, what you saw at the time.

Now change your dominant position, raise your left leg if you are left handed or right leg if you are right handed, keep balancing notice how uneasy you feel, uncomfortable, as though you might fall over. Now step outside of the box.

Step Up

What does it now mean to Step Up?

Psychologically to change any pattern of behaviour, for that action to become a habit requires continuous practice for at least thirty days.

Stand Out

Our society is very competitive, so many people applying for the same positions or competing for the same clients. What is so unique about you, that you will be noticed?

Think about Virgin, Oprah, Apple, Starbucks, McDonald's Microsoft and Dell. What do you know about them? Why do you remember so much?

These companies have been able to build their identity so strong that they are easily recognised and they build a loyal following of customers. This is referred to as building a brand. A product or service that can be easily recognised from the thousands of other competing products.

How will you stand out?

My Action Points

1. What is bothering or annoying you at the moment? What excites you and gets you pumped up, make a list? Against at each point give a reason why.

2. Paint a picture of what you see. Cut out photos from your favourite magazines and put them together in a scrapbook. Call it your DREAMBOOK.

3. Write a list of all the things you want for your life, start with the tangible but also think about the stuff money cannot buy. Review your notes in chapter 1.

Start it like this:

I want………...........................because it will……..…...……………

I want…...……….................because I can give.........……………..

I want ………...............because I will feel. ……….....…………..

I want to ………..............in. … months because I can see

………....……..…...

I want to ……..............in …….....months because I can hear

………....……...…...

My Action Points

I want to do ………………… ….before I die to ……......……….…..

I want to become…………...............because..........................………….

I want to be ……….............and ………......................….....…………..

I want to ……….............to leave ……......................….....………….

I shall ……………………………….before I retire so that my family

can..

When I reach the age of retirement I will be ……………………….

……………………………………………………………………………….

29

3 Get Up and Face Reality

**Don't be afraid of the space between your dreams and reality.
If you can dream it, you can make it. (Belva Davis)**

What are the realities facing you in your life? Are you overwhelmed, burdened or just plane stuck? A feeling of being stuck and no matter how hard you think or try, you cannot see a way out.

Something is Wrong With the Scale

I can recall times when I felt a bit on the fat side. Stepped onto the scale to weigh myself and wondered why the needle was moving so fast. I can remember shouting to my wife, "Sharon, something is wrong with the scale, where is the new one you bought?" Sharon said, "There is nothing wrong with the scale, it's a brand new one, stop eating so much cake".

The scales never paint the picture you want to see but they do not lie. For it to be just right you are going to have to do some work, burn off some calories and cut back on munching and eat proper meals. As I said, "Work".

To recognise where we are we must take stock, face the realities one by one and deal with them.

Taking Stock

Borrowing from the world of business, taking stock, in its original form is the verification of the amount and condition of the goods, perishable or non-perishable, held by a business for further processing or resale to the public.

It costs to hold stock, whether in a warehouse or office space it has to be purchased, so retailers try not to hold too much but just enough to meet the demands of customers. The Japanese developed the concept of Just in Time stock control, goods delivered from suppliers only when needed.

There are times in our lives when we have failed to take a break from the treadmill of routines. We are running and doing for the sake of it, not really remembering why we are doing what we do in the first place. Two, three years later it is just another routine, it has become obsolete, stock that needs destroying.

You Cannot Sell Substandard Goods

You cannot sell substandard goods or products to customers or if you did, you would not have any customers left to sell to. Businesses of all sizes invest large amounts of money in trained staff and technology to monitor and determine whether stock is damaged, obsolete or out of date. Based on the findings the stock is either replaced or sold cheaply.

A lot of the stock discarded by businesses end up in street markets and car boot sales across the country.

Get Up and Wash Your Face

Every day you wake up and carry out a number of routines without thinking about them. Get up and wash your face, shower and dress, have breakfast, drive, walk or take the bus to work.

Arrive at work, have coffee, chat with colleagues and turn on the computer to read post.

You may have a different order but you understand the gist. Your brain has been programmed to accept these as normal, without question.

What colour was the toothpaste?

Our brain skips over the everyday routines being performed as unimportant to remember. Ask yourself what side of the bed you got up? What colour was the toothpaste? Did you plan your route to work?

So much of our lives disappear in front of us because we are not paying attention to the activities we deem unimportant in our subconscious mind.

Now that was just an average day in your life, what have you done in the last twelve months, year or decade to take stock of your own life? Aren't you valuable or precious?

Is your life worth evaluating? How do you know if you are wasting time, if you have not spent the time to take stock?

Everything you do is costing you time and money. Either opportunities forgone, lost forever that would have made you money. Time lost that you cannot recover from the past.

It is time to take stock of your life, to measure, assess and evaluate where there is room for improvement and development.

The entrepreneur always searches for change, responds to it, and exploits it as an opportunity.
(Peter Drucker (Biz Quotes)

Change is about altering the content or the features of an object or returning something to its original form. You have probably spent your lifetime changing your clothes, your home, your partners and still feeling dissatisfied with the outcome.

Blaming others always seems like an answer in the short term but in the long run someone has to take responsibility for what needs to be done. That person has to be you. Changing from the inside out so that every aspect of life is affected.. What is it called?

Identify some areas in your life that you would like to change. Use the following categories as an example.

1. Family
2. Personal Development
3. Finances
4. Health
5. Faith
6. Lifestyle
7. Friendships

Make some notes.

Transforming Your Reality

> **Man, alone, has the power to transform his thoughts into physical reality; man, alone, can dream and make his dreams come true.   (Napoleon Hill)**

Transformation means to change in form, appearance or structure, which is to metamorphose. Metamorphosis is a change in the form and often habits of an animal during normal development after the embryonic stage. In insects we see the transformation of a maggot into an adult fly and a caterpillar into a butterfly. (*Wikipedia*)

We are all seeking some change in our lives, looking for perfection or the best at all times to create a new reality.

It is not obvious to the eye that something ugly can become something beautiful. We tend to see things the way they are and no better. Not realising it can be metamorphosis right in front of your eyes.

Think of the caterpillar that crawls on the ground even risks being crushed that one-day becomes a butterfly, a creature of such beauty. Muhammad Ali once said that he "Floats like a butterfly and sting like a bee".

The greatest challenge is not just to recognise that change is required but the transformation you seek requires a process.

In the last chapter you reviewed your life and said how it could be improved but to bring transformational change you must understand the cycle of change.

James Prochaska and Carlo DiClemente developed this model of change as a process. *(Solution Focused Coaching 2003).*

They recognised six stages to the process;

1)   Pre-contemplation - this is before we start to think about change, it is like doodling, worrying about the change before you even think about it. Refer to fig.3.1.

2)   Contemplation - this is when we start to think about change, wanting things to change but at the same time wanting to keep what we have, total feeling of ambivalence.

3)   Preparation Stage - we have made the decision to change. Something has pushed us to this point and we are fed up with the norm as we see it before, even though still uncertain.

4)   Action - these are the steps identified in the process.

5)   Maintenance - this is where the new actions are part of our behaviour patterning that needed to be maintained. We either fail or succeed at this point and

will exit or try again.

6)   Relapse - back where we started, doing the very thing
      we wanted to change so hard. But this is normal in
      everyday life to relapse and then start the cycle again.

When someone slips it requires greater effect to restart the
cycle to get back on track so requiring a lot of support. For
example those suffering from addictions, alcoholic and drug
abuse which are extreme examples.

What about the last time you tried to get fit and went to the
gym, you probably slipped before the month was over.

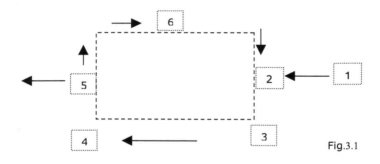

Fig.3.1

Now think about your own life and the different things you
want to change for example, losing weight, changing jobs
and going back into education. Map out this process from 1
to 6.

    1. Pre-contemplation
        What have you been itching about?

2. Contemplation
   What have you been contemplating to change?

3. Preparation Stage
   You have made the decision to change and now working through it. Make a note of the change.

   Action
   What actions have you taken or planned?

4. Maintenance
   How do you propose to maintain this new behaviour?

5. Relapse

   What safety mechanisms have you put in place to prevent relapse? If you do how will you recover?

What You Believe Shapes Your Reality

What you believe shapes your norms and values that guide your life.

It took me a long time to get to the point of my life where my reality was a true reflection of me, not being shaped by others. Formal education has a way of channelling you down a particular path where you feel unable to change or take a detour.

Let me explain, for those of you who did GCSE's, the bright ones or "goodie, goodies" worked hard all year, did all the assignments and the teachers felt confident they would pass. While there were others "baddies" who only worked just before the exams, "swat", learning like a parrot, not too sure if they would pass the exams but managing to pull through by "the skin of their teeth", lastminute.com.

> Those who worked hard and those who did

The "baddies" were bored with the traditional way of learning, normal routine of school and would have probably excelled in a different environment.

This signalled the beginning of the treadmill of further study for A' levels, then work or university. If you opted for work at the first opportunity then it was the uphill struggle for promotion, more pay, further study just to climb.

Pursuing the dream life or that you were lead to believe the dream were the symbols of success.

> *What you believe shapes what you think, what you think determines your actions, how you act informs people of the person you have become*

What do you do? "STOP", "STOP"

I never stopped to ask myself if I was enjoying this. Fighting to get to the top only to realise the ladder (job, career, company) is against the wrong wall, too frightened to get off because the bills have to be paid, mortgage, car loans etc., for the lifestyle you think you need.

Stop Before You Hurt Yourself

Before you get a heart attack or burn a valve ask yourself these questions;

1. What am I doing with my life?

2. Where am I really heading?

3. Why am I on this path?

4. How do I adjust course?

I do not expect you to have any conclusive answers right now, just say them out aloud, and be sure to be somewhere where you will not disturb anyone.

Do you feel invincible?

The younger you are, the more invincible you will feel, not really taking into account how life is quickly passing by. You feel like superman, heading for the next crisis ready to save or be saved.

Review what you have done so far, the education you have had, the relationships you have built, the activities you have engaged in, the fun you have had or not had, the places you have been or not been.

Scribble on a blank sheet of paper what you are thinking, as it comes, no order. Spend about 20–30 minutes just off-loading.

Now make a list of all these thoughts. They are your thoughts so there are no wrong or right answers, it is about you.

Against each thought write how you see it developing in the future. Now review what you have written and then giving each a rating in terms of importance to you on a scale of 1-10; being clear about what you see and how you feel.

We started the chapter talking about change, what we want is real transformation. We often feel change is a long process and sometimes unobtainable in our own lives.

Have you ever thought of how often the traffic lights change?

Red, Green, Amber, you sit waiting for the change so you can go forward. How long have you been waiting for your change?

Whatever change you are looking for, it is only a thought away. Whatsoever you think you can become. It is one thought away, all you have to do is act. But you may be interpreting the signals incorrectly, you may be waiting for someone to give you the green light or red just seems to last for ever.

In preparing you for this change, waiting for the lights to change, you must know what you want in each area of your life. Most often we know exactly what we don't want but not spent enough time on what we do want.

In scripture, a man sat at the poolside waiting for a miracle for over thirty-eight years, never managed to get in the pool on time for his breakthrough. When Jesus asked him what he wanted he never knew.

Excuses Will Void Your Opportunities

The man at the pool was full of excuses so he almost missed his opportunity. Are you still making excuses because you are not sure what you want?

Preparing for Battle

You are often not sure how to deal with the obstacles that you face. You are unprepared because you have never seen the situation before or you have not spent enough time thinking about what you must do. I call it preparing for the battle for life.

How do we prepare for the battle for life?

Pilots are trained in simulator machines that make the situation seem real. Learning about the controls and preparing the mind to respond to all possible situations.

Pilots learn to fly because they want to. They learn to master the plane in all weather conditions before they carry

40

any passengers. Once training is completed they gain experience practising on that strength.

Most people do not know what their strengths are. When you ask them, they look at you with a blank stare, or they respond in terms of subject knowledge,which is the wrong answer.
(Peter Drucker)

Identify Your Strengths

The key is to work from your strengths, the gifts, abilities and talents that you possess. Find out what you are naturally good at and develop it. In the book Now Discover Your Strengths the authors Marcus Buckingham and Donald Clifton embark on what they call the strength revolution.

Strength Revolution

Encouraging organisations to capitalise on the differences between employees, identify their natural talents and develop those talents so they are transformed into bona fide strengths.

The book describes a set of language that describes your strengths i.e. The Achiever, The Activator, The Arranger and a number of other dominant traits. They developed a Strength Finder Profile test to help you identify your strengths. Go to www.strengthfinder.com and take the test.

Once you have discovered your strength profile you are able to work to your own advantage and get the necessary help you need in all other areas you lack competence.

Your Own SWOT Analysis

Strengths	Weakness
Opportunities	Threats

The SWOT analysis has been around for some time and you may have thought you have exhausted its use.

- Strengths

  What we think we are good at

- Weaknesses

  The things we struggle to do, not good at

- Opportunities

  Deals, events, relationships that will change our lives or add value.

- Threats

  Anything that will bring harm to ourselves or business, destroy it, is a threat.

Make a complete list in each of these SWOT areas.

Now consider your strengths, what you are good at that can provide a solution to what you are facing in your T.O.W (Threats, Opportunities and Weaknesses).

Consider your response as a matrix, each strength along the horizontal axis explaining how it will effect a weakness or explore an opportunity.

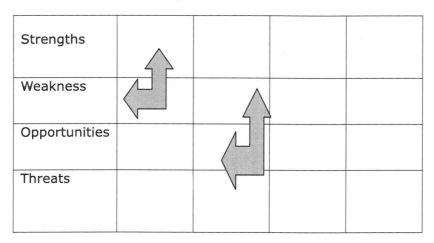

Strengths				
Weakness				
Opportunities				
Threats				

What would you recommend in this case?

	Strengths	Weaknesses
1	Public speaker	Unable to right clearly
2	Excellent planner	Poor implementer

My Action Points

1. Make a list of all the excuses you can think of, the reasons why you cannot do something.

   I cannot

   I will not

   I should not

My Action Points

I must not

Now re-write your list without the "not" and read them out loud.

2. Create an ideal picture of what life could be like. Review the main areas of your life that is important to you and record:

    •   What they could look like

    •   How your feelings have changed

    •   What you hear

4 Be Enthusiastic About Life

A man can succeed at almost anything for
which he has unlimited enthusiasm
(Charles Schwab)

Enthusiasm is defined as a feeling of excitement, overflowing with eager enjoyment and approval. It is the sign or expression of someone having fun.

It acts like fuel. Imagine being in the driving seat of a Ferrari, ready to go, anticipating the drive, the power, the force that you are about to experience. You turn the key in the ignition and the sound of the car fills the atmosphere. That is exactly what excitement does; it fills the atmosphere and creates an expectation.

We carry a power of enablement to share with our Gifts, Abilities and Talents. To make a contribution to the society in which we live.

The Prime Minister calls it the Big Society. This is not a new concept as our communities are held together by the unpaid contributions of thousands of individuals. Their enthusiasm makes the lives of the recipients of their work liveable. The homeless, the disabled, the broken-hearted, the sick and so much more are impacted by the excitement of just a few. These stories impact real lives, have you got a story to tell?

Nothing guarantees success in life other than the enthusiasm you carry that others see and feel.

Enthusiasm is one of the most powerful engines of success. When you do a thing, do it with all your might. Put your whole soul into it. Stamp it with your own personality. Be active, be energetic, be enthusiastic and helpful, and you will accomplish your object. Nothing great was ever achieved without enthusiasm. (Ralph Waldo Emerson)

A Heart of Gold

The world was drawn to Nelson Mandela because of his enthusiasm for life. He suffered in jail for 25 years and on his release he faced the world with a smile on his face and a heart so big it could hold everyone and still had room.

Enthusiasm is like electricity, as a source of energy the effect goes far and wide and is seen by all. This form of energy comes from the soul. It cannot be purchased or imitated, it is a spiritual connection.

Like current flowing in an appliance it needs to have a focus. Enthusiasm requires a goal, an intended destination one that you are able to visualise or have a sense of feeling for. How would you feel if you bought your dream car or house? How would you feel if you were booked on an all-expenses paid world tour?

Think about it for a second. What do you want right now that if it happened tomorrow it would get you excited?

Get that picture and place it on your wall, desk or fridge so that you will see it every day. Tell yourself it's going to happen as you picture the event in your mind.

Passion

What would you do tomorrow even if you were not being paid? What would you like to do every day if you had all the money you required and did not have to work?

Passion is like the purr of the power of the engine underneath the bonnet of a Porsche, a Jaguar or BMW. Whatever you consider to be powerful and able to be self-propelled.

The dictionary sees Passion as the trait of being intensely emotional; any object of warmth, affection or devotion; a strong feeling or emotion; an irrational but irresistible motive for a belief or action.

It is an irresistible desire to act in a particular way that will make you move mountains, walk around or climb over, when everything else is going against you. It is the conviction you sense to act that you must follow.

Passion is Like Your Car

The car has the ability to accelerate and de-accelerate and maintain motion regardless of the weather conditions. The car moves in whatever direction the driver decides, or stops when the driver decides to. You have the ability to respond to life with an intuition that comes from your heart, out of your heart flows the thoughts, concerns and issues.

It starts when you decide to and stops when you decide not to. It gives you an invincible power to act now.

A great idea may keep you motivated for a few weeks but having passion for a particular cause or concern, a Big Holy Audacious Goal will keep you fired up.
People listen to passionate speakers, passionate politicians, passionate entrepreneurs, passionate doctors or passionate teachers, it can apply to any discipline or person.

Passion is a critical element for anyone who wants to achieve a dream. Why? Because it is the starting point of all achievement.
(John Maxwell)

Wear your passion at all times so the world can see what

47

you are about, hear what you have to say and might join you in your cause.

What does passion do for anyone?

Builds your confidence for expressing how you feel

No matter how someone belittles your idea, if you are passionate about your idea, cause and business, they will not discourage you.

Generates and mobilises action

Faith without any form of action is no faith at all. Action has to be a fruit of faith. Passion not only generates action but helps to sustain action over a long period of time even when all the evidence is against you, your passion is working.

Gives you a sense of direction

A sense of direction is a must in acting upon an idea or cause. This inner strength will drive the direction and keep the focus on the things that matter.

Passion Withstands Rejection

It takes a strong heart to keep going when the "No's" outnumber the "Yes's".

Now the big question is, "how do you identify your passion or what are you passionate about?" Well, let us see how you respond to the following questions:

1. What gets you heated or fired up?

2. What gets you annoyed so much that you must take action?

3. What gets you excited?

4. What do you want to change?

5. What solutions do you think about all the time?

6. Why do you feel you must take action?

My Action Points

- Now review your answers to the above questions.

- Ask two of your closest friends the same questions about you and record their response.

- After reviewing all the information you have gathered make commitment to act on each point.

5 The Million Pound Asset

You can be anything you want to be if only you believe with sufficient conviction and act in accordance with your faith; for whatever the mind can conceive and believe, the mind can achieve.   (Napoleon Hill)

Your Childhood Imagination

There are so many things that you did as a child which were wonderful memories but others you do not want to recall at all because they bring great pain.

I do not want to bring you back to a painful time of your life but I want you to go back through the memory archives and pull out the memorable events in your life that made you smile.

Your imaginary world

You invented games, your own imaginary world of Cowboys and Indians, Jesse James, Lone Ranger, Thunderbirds. You would act out these roles with great imagination. Driving an imaginary car or truck or flying an imaginary plane.

What can you remember as a child that formed your imaginary world? Think about it for two or three minutes.

Imagination is more important than knowledge.
Knowledge is limited. Imagination encircles the world.
(Albert Einstein)

As child you are expected to do as you are told and not ask "why". This used to be my favourite word:

"Wash your face", "why?"

"Go to bed", why?

"Get up to go to School", why?

"Do your homework", why?

"Study", why?

"Be a good boy", why?

Children always look for a reason to do things and this is a wonderful attitude to have because it can help frame your world. For your parents it was a pain in the "   ".

Having to explain to a four year old in a hurry; unable to get anything done because of a curious mind can slow you down. But it is at these formative years that children show signs of what they might become. Their inquisitive minds testing everything in sight.

What if parents took more time out of their busy schedules to guide those young minds with great imagination?

What you believe shapes your attitude

Your belief system controls your expectations of life. You can become anything you want to, providing you first believe. When you believe you must:

- Make a Decision
- Choose which way to go
- Do it

Making a decision to act is you contemplating what to do, weighing up the advantages against the disadvantages; the benefits to be derived from your decision. Once you have built your case in your own mind, then nothing should change your mind.

There is a saying – People don't care how much you know until they know how much you care.

Attitude Determines the Outcome

Our attitude determines the outcome in every situation that we find ourselves. Muhammed Ali was a great boxer not just with the gloves on but in his mind. Consequently he had a great attitude. He once said that some people came to see him win, some came to see him get beaten, but either way it was a full house, all the seats were taken.

> Any fact facing us is not as important as our attitude
> toward it, for that determines our success or failure
> (Norman Vincent Peale)

The ability to respond with a positive attitude to every situation is developed over time. In its basic form an attitude is a response which you can change at any time. In the same way one develops a habit by practising a particular activity

People Charged to Profit and Loss

The accounts of most organisations have a profit and loss account or income and expenditure showing all the things they have bought or expensed throughout a twelve month period. This is what we call charged to the profit and loss account. Among these items are the costs of the people who make the business work every day, year on year.

In the balance sheet there are tangible assets and intangible assets. Assets are costs that bring a benefit of more than one year over its useful life, like computers, furniture and intellectual property. So by that definition alone, where should you charge the staff costs?

The benefit to be derived from employing people can be

derived over a long period of time. Hence by definition of an asset they should be carried in the balance sheet.

Consequently staff are treated with a very short-term attitude, they can always be easily replaced. But that is wrong.

It takes years and costs thousands of pounds to find the right staff and to train them to meet the needs of the company. They are therefore not easily replaceable; there is always a cost.

What is the greatest asset in any organisation? Think about all the activities or tasks that get done, the Key Performance Indicators.

1. Ideas generated by people
2. Products produced by people
3. Solutions created by people
4. Relationships created among people
5. Warm environment created by people
6. Profits generated by people.

Have you yet thought of an answer?

Who performs all of the above in your organisation? What would happen if the key points listed were not done?

The continued benefit to be derived by an organisation is the development of those minds in the application of their Giftings, Abilities and Talents to create the goods and services that the organisation needs to deliver good service and compete in the marketplace.

To Change A Person Work on The Heart

The brain is the central control for our nervous system giving out and receiving thousands of instructions second by second. But the heart pumps the food, the oxygen that we need and feeds the brain. Who is more powerful the brain or the heart?

All life begins with the heart, so to get the results we are looking for, to get a better individual, a kinder more caring person we cannot ignore the heart.

How do we reduce our crime rate?
How do we reduce the prison culture?
How do we stop people going to jail?
How do we help a generation of hopelessness?

You have the power to create...............

You have the power to create anything you put your mind to, if you do not believe then revisit chapter one, The World of Big Dreamers.

Where does it begin?

It begins with an idea. A thought or suggestion about a possible course of action. A mental impression, a belief. (Oxford English Dictionary).

Your idea is your "Eureka" moment. Life changing at least to you initially.

Think about it, good ideas:

- Anita Roddick - Body Shop
- Dyson – Bagless hoover
- 3M – Post it notes
- Ikea – Self assemble furniture
- Amazon – Books and digital products
- Virgin – Airways, Records
- Apple – Iphone, Ipad, Imac
- Microsoft – Software
- Mary Kay - Cosmetics

What triggers these ideas in the minds of people? Taking time to think, focus on developing things is a start. There is no set place to get ideas to flow but whatever you feel comfortable with, try it.

- Quiet spot
- Special chair
- Holiday
- Brainstorming session
- Being airborne
- Walk
- Ride
- Golf
- Badminton
- Tennis
- Seminar / workshop

The key is to recognise what you are thinking, whether dissatisfied with a service or product or a gap you see in the market.

The million pound question is what have you done about your idea?

Experts Say No but Your Heart Says Yes

A friend said it will never work
You thought it was rubbish
The experts said it will not work
Your bank manager said it cannot work.

Regardless of what other people are saying what are you thinking about your idea?

The greatest detriment to many people's success tomorrow is their thinking today. If their thinking is limited, so is their potential. But if people can keep growing in their thinking, they will constantly outgrow what they are doing. And their potential will always be off the charts.   (John Maxwell)

Changed thinking is the key to success but you have to work at it. It is not an automatic process, it is a habit that needs developing. It requires an investment of time and money but the rewards can be greater.

Stock markets crash, property markets also crash as we have seen ourselves, but a human mind with the ability to think well, is like a diamond mine that never runs out.

My Action Points

1. Describe your contribution to your organisation to date.

2. How would you like to develop your contribution?

3. Are you being adequately compensated for what you do, give reasons.

4. What reward would you expect in your ideal position within the organisation?

The Power of Why?

It is said that the Polaroid camera was invented because a child asked why. In 1943 Edwin Land suggested to his three year old daughter that they take the camera film to the shop for processing which would take a week to process. She asked, "Why do I have to wait to see my picture?"

The 5 whys technique was developed by Toyota in the 1970's to deal with the cause of manufacturing problems rather than treat symptoms; breaking down market opportunities to generate further insight.

Why do you want to leave your job?

Because I am not being challenged on a daily basis.

Why?

Because I have been doing this job for over ten years.

Why?

Change [of?] direction.

Why?

I can work when I want to.

Why?

Be there for my family.

Use this technique with any of your ideas or decisions..

You must remember that most ideas are not brand new; they are variations of an existing idea that has been improved, changed or modified in some way.

Think about:

Dyson vs. Hoover

Virgin Airways vs. British Airways

Colgate toothpaste vs. Sensidine

Barclays Bank vs. Natwest Bank

How to generate new ideas?

As we said earlier most ideas are a variation of an original idea.

Ask yourself these questions:

1. What product or service can I adapt?
   (Adapt)

2. How could I modify it?
   (Modify)

3. How could I add to this product?
   (Magnify)

4. What could I take away?
   (Minify)

5. What could I use instead?
   (Substitute)

6. How could I alter the composition?
   (Rearrange)

7. How could I turn the product or service around?
   (Reverse)

8. What could I put together to make a new one?
   (Combine)

6   You Were Born To Work

Man was designed for accomplishment, that is you, engineered for success and endowed with the seeds of greatness.
(Zig Ziglar)

Work in the western world has been defined as something we do from 9 to 5, five or seven days a week for forty or fifty years. Each day you exchange your time for the promise of money.

At the end of the week or month you are compensated for your time. You are encouraged to get a good education so that you can get a good job to earn a good salary to live a good life.

In the printing industry each piece of work is a job. A job is a set of tasks that form your job description, the position that you get paid for regardless of how talented you may be.

Work you were
born to do

What defines you?

Ask someone who they are and what they do, they will define themselves by the role or job they perform each day. So someone's perception of you is determined by your job. Imagine if you do not enjoy what you are doing? Imagine if your job is seen as boring, what happens to you?

From the age of industrialisation workers worked in one job until they retired. Totally secured they would not be unemployed. But that has changed significantly in the last ten years. The expectation is that you will now hold a number of roles during your working age.

Nick Williams, the founder of the Heart At Work Project, in his book, "The Work We Were Born To Do" states that work comes from within; it is about being engaged, where we choose to channel our life's energy.

It has the ability to link the everyday and mundane to our heart and soul. Connecting what we do with our desire for deeper meaning and purpose. It is the big picture encompassing the why and not just what. Work provides the opportunity to find and express our genius, be an inspiration and discover you. Work is bigger than the job you do while creating your work.

Work should provide you with five basic essentials for your life
- Satisfaction
- Expression
- Reconnection
- Value
- Entertainment

Satisfaction

Whether you are serving the congregation on Sunday with words of wisdom and reconnecting their sprits or serving customers in a retail store providing the goods. They may be your clients purchasing your technical skills or knowledge.

The irony is the congregation on Sunday is your client or customers on Monday. The level of satisfaction you provide should always be at its best; aiming to satisfy at all times.

Expression

Work expresses who you are and affords you the opportunity to share what you have with the world and make your contribution to the community in which you choose to live. Your Giftings, Abilities and Talent determine that contribution and help you to engage with others.

Les Brown in one of his seminars talked about being at the end of your life, about to go, standing around you are three friends you've had all your life, Giftings, Abilities and Talent.

They are moaning at you, Giftings, "I could not come alive because you stopped me, you never recognised me". Abilities shouting, "you never put me to the test and now I am about to die with you". Talent is devastated, "I cannot touch another generation. You never took the opportunities in front of you to expose me to the world".

Can you imagine the number of gifted and talented people with extraordinary abilities who have ignored the pulse of their heartstrings and not aligned themselves with the calling on their lives? What they feel they were called to do. This calling is something you sense at times when the routines are making you wary and you feel this is not what you should be doing.

Reconnection

Reconnecting with people and engaging in the tasks and daily routines constitutes living. Unless you choose to become a hermit and live without human contact or interface, work is your connection point, it keeps the reality real.

One of my heroes is Stevie Wonder, blind all his life but able to write music, plays instruments and sings his heartstrings. He could have done a number of jobs in his life. Are you singing the songs from your heart?

The Power of His Imagination to See and Feel

You see the legend, Stevie has become as an artist, producer and songwriter, and you know that was what he was born to do. The only thing that he could rely on was the power of his imagination to see and feel his direction.

How do you then connect with what you were born to do?

It is so easy to talk about what we do not want. We know what it looks like, what it sounds like and even where it lives. We are able to spell it out to the umpteenth degree. But ask us what we do want and the silence starts.

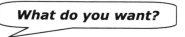

What do you want?

Your heart speaks louder than words. The inner voice that shouts out every so often, always ignored, is waiting for you to tune in. Ask yourself the question every day for a week, **what do I want**? Then look out for your answers, they will show up.

You attract what you speak into. Whatsoever your interests are, that brings excitement to your life, speak about those things, let them become the centre of your thoughts, and watch out.

Over the years I never believed that anyone really listened to me until I heard my wife repeat my words as quotes. Can you imagine, Alex says, "   ". For the first time it shocked me so much that my words were being listened to.

Never underestimate what you have to say.

Listen to the people in your life. Other people have a way of seeing things in you that you do not easily recognise. Living with you every day, you take yourself for granted and become very dismissive of your own thoughts and abilities.

Value

Your sense of value is derived by what you love or enjoy doing. But you may ask, What if I don't love my job? The value you derive is probably attached to what you are able to purchase. The sense of value gives fulfilment and satisfaction.

Spend a few moments and give this some thought.

Do you feel valued in what you do? If not, why not?

....

....

How does your contribution make a difference?

....

....

Entertainment

We started by talking about the length of time we spend working, it never stops. Your entire life is spent working paid or unpaid. Therefore work should be able to put a smile on your face or the face of those you serve.

My Action Points

Now think about the work you do and answer the following questions truthfully.

1) What degree of Satisfaction am I deriving from work, is this really me?

2) Am I expressing myself in this role? Am I best suited to something else?

3) How is this role helping me to reconnect with people in my community?

4) What Value do I place on what I am doing? Do I feel valued?

5) Do I feel entertained? Do I put a smile on the face of others in my role?

Provide a rating for each of these points, 1 to 20, 1 being the lowest, 10 being at tolerance levels, 20 being the highest.

If you score:

50 and below - you need to completely change direction.

51–70 - you need to re-evaluate what you are doing.

70 and above - there is room for improvement.

7 Focus

The same thinking that has led you to where you are
is not going to lead you to where you want to go.
(Albert Einstein)

We live in a very busy world. Our lives are not our own,
we share everything we have whether we have a family or
not. There is always something competing for your attention
and your time. From the moment you wake, getting ready
for work, arriving at work and performing the role you get
paid to do there is not enough of you to do all that is to be
done.

Your Time is a Precious Resource
That is to be used wisely

Time is the most precious resource that we have and we
must learn to manage, value and dispense it wisely.

We all have a personal, spiritual and emotional bank that
registers our activities. We give and receive into that bank;
transactions are taking place every second of our life
through the currency of time.

Scripture tells us that there is a time for everything under
the sun; time to build, to be born, to die. Our greatest
challenge is once we arrive on earth we have no idea how
much time we have on this planet. So the clock starts
ticking straight away from the moment the doctor slaps you
to welcome you into the world.

The question we should always be asking ourselves is one of importance, is this activity important to me? Does it add value to my life?

Does it add value?

Determining the level of importance creates a need to measure the impact on your life. Only that which fits what we are looking for and want to get involved with should be affecting us.

You must know why you do what you do, which requires that you understand the purpose and value of all that you do.
(Tony Jeary)

Always ask yourself is it:

- Beneficial to my life and family?
- Advantageous to where I am going?
- Necessary for my journey?
- Key to the steps I need to take?

Value is therefore deposited or withdrawn from your bank by your daily existence. What is the state of your bank balance?

Did you notice the effect of the convergence of the light, the raw heat harnessed to one central point?

Have you ever sat outside on a sunny day with a mirror and captured the rays of the sun to one central point?

Did you notice the effect of the convergence of the light, the raw heat harnessed to one central point? The intensity of the heat burns the object that the heat is diverted to. This is called the power of focus. Concentrating so much energy to a small manageable area lights the fire within us to make something happen.

There is something about getting the idea off the ground,

making it work in small manageable chunks. A small win in a short period of time builds momentum.

I used to like flying kites when I was around 9 to 11 years old. I would lay the kite on the ground, straighten the cord, tie it to the kite and run with all my energy. Run and run until the wind caught hold of the kite. The kite would then start to rise with me hanging on to the cord desperate not to let it go. A true sense of satisfaction for making it fly.

What are you flying?

The ability to fly requires concentrated effort, no distractions and the eagerness anxiety attached to making something happen. Are you overloaded doing too many things at once?

Pare-to Principle

An Italian economist Vildredo Pareto observed that 80% of income in Italy went to 20% of the population. Pareto then carried out surveys on a number of other countries. He found that wealth is concentrated in an even smaller percentage of individuals.

It became a common rule of thumb in business; "80% of your production comes from 20% of your staff".

Consider your daily routines at work, according to this rule out of a full day at work only 20% of what you do is generating any real results. Part of your time is spent doing a number of irrecoverable, low value activities. That means 80% of your time is non-productive. What do you do with the non-productive part?

Let us expand this further, 20% of the workforce is producing 80% of the results. That is why companies go through periods of downsizing, trying to minimise the non-productive element.

In your personal life the rule is applicable. 80% of your time is being spent on things that others could do, leaving you more time for the 20% of thinks you need to do.

We can use this principle to help us concentrate on the things we want for our lives more effectively and manage down the non-productive parts.

How do you focus?

The main steps that come to mind is:

- Recognise the need to focus
- Understand the Why
- Set aside time
- Determine what form it will take
- Test the plan
- Execute the plan

Recognise the Need to Focus

This coincides with the wants in your life. Whatever you want to do or wherever you want to go so strongly that it becomes a goal, should become your target. Another way of describing it is your burning desire. Ready, steady, aim and fire.

Understand the Why

If a desired result is deemed life threatening it becomes the dominant thought. For example, raising funds for a cancer operation, or a rare blood disease. But any desire that is not a burning one will fade.

Set aside time

Create a space in your busy schedule to allow time and space for your creative genius, visualise and explore your thoughts.

Determine what form it will take

Some people think best in complete silence while others are able to think while ironing, playing golf, washing or even reading. What is important is to find the best method that will work for you.

Test the plan

The first time you intentionally take time out, you might feel very uncomfortable but just do it. Remember a habit forms after thirty days of practising an activity.

Execute the plan

After the initial test run, keep it short and in manageable chunks of time slots. You will begin to see amazing results in your creativity.

My Action Points

Make a list of ten things that you must do today.

1)

2)

3)

4)

5)

6)

My Action Points

7)

8)

9)

10)

Now cross off the things that do not meet the profile of your BANK;

Beneficial, Advantageous, Necessary, Key.

For each point above that meets your profile make a note of how it is;

    ⅄   Beneficial

    ⅄   Advantageous

➤ Necessary

➤ Key

8 Build Your Team

You need to be aware of what others are doing, applaud their efforts, acknowledge their successes, and encourage them in their pursuits. When we all help one another, everybody wins.
(Jim Stovali (Biz Quote))

There is a saying that no man is an island. No matter how good you are there will be a point when you require the help of others.

If you consider the development of Western economies over the last hundred years you will see how we grew from a pre-industrial era growing our own food to the industrial revolution, the mass production of goods in factories. We are more dependent on each other than we have ever been.

There is a definition that has become widely accepted among trainers;

Together
Everyone
Achieves
More

It implies that more can be done or we can increase our performance if we reduce a task or activity into smaller manageable parts.

Consequently a major project can be broken down into a number of mini-projects

Each part becomes a specialist area with clearly defined responsibilities and roles. Consequently a major project can be broken down into a number of mini-projects with their own individual time frame for completion.

A team should always seek to be very clear in its communication, bringing the right people together who share a similar cause or purpose heading towards the same goal.

The concept of working in teams is not new but human tendency is to try and work all alone.

Tuck man's model of team development looks at four key stages of bringing a team together;

- ⅄ Forming
- ⅄ Storming
- ⅄ Norming
- ⅄ Performing

These stages are not to be ignored when putting teams together.

In the forming stage people are trying to find where they fit. Storming irons out all the rough edges and members may decide to quit. Norming and Performing is where the work starts to get done as people adjust to each other's style of working.

What are some of the benefits of working with a team?

- ⅄ Share workload
- ⅄ Planning more effective
- ⅄ Brain storm together
- ⅄ Able to spot gaps
- ⅄ Greater combined effort
- ⅄ Economies of scale

What are some of the disadvantages of working with a team?

- ⅄ Waiting for others to catch up
- ⅄ Lack of clarity in roles prevents completion of tasks
- ⅄ Clash of personalities
- ⅄ Discord among team members

What type of leader are you?

The style of leadership will normally determine how the team operates, how well each person integrate as a team. John Adair looks at the styles of leadership in terms of whether you are:

(A)	Autocratic	-	Tell not ask
(D)	Democratic	-	Encourage choice
(T)	Transactional	-	Exchange, job, money
(E)	Enabling	-	Inspiring with vision
(C)	Controlling	-	Manipulation
(Ch)	Charismatic	-	Personality to inspire
(NC)	Non–Charismatic	-	Knowledge and analytical

So what is your basic style?

Are you enthusiastic, confident, tough, warm, humble, and able to listen?

One of the most influential team models that I have come across is that by Belbin. He describes nine different personality types to make up your team:

1.	Plant	-	Creative
2.	Co-ordinator	-	Confident, decision maker
3.	Monitor	-	Strategic, accurate
4.	Implementer	-	Disciplined
5.	Complete Finisher	-	Delivers on time
6.	Resource Investigator	-	Enthusiast, networker
7.	Shaper	-	Challenging, driven

8. Team worker   -   Diplomatic
9. Specialist   -   Self-starter

This is not a general rule but it is good to see who you are working with and how best to manage. From my own observations in life and business, you need to decide who are the essential people you require to make things work, key people that have no roles, useful but not essential and the ideal members if all was in place.

When you are starting out with a lack of money you need to have the basics;

- Creator – Coach
- Analyst - Accountant
- Solicitor
- Helper

The saying is that Cash is King. If a business runs out of cash then it is in serious trouble. Well if you do not have these people in your team then you will soon be out of business.

The creator would normally be yourself as it is your idea but you do need a coach to help you to navigate your journey. If you cannot afford one then try a mentor who is unpaid.

The accountant is your analyst, an analytical mind is required to make sure the numbers are correct and to direct and measure the financial position at any point in time.

The solicitor is required to help you navigate the law, stay on the right side.

Helpers are every kind of help that you may need which can be contracted for short periods of time until the phase is complete.

When the business has been trading for a number of years and there is a need to strengthen the team, consider these:

1. Dreamer   -   The Visionary
2. Realist   -   Brings things back to earth
3. Expert   -   Knowledge needed for key areas
4. Achiever   -   Stretches the team, driven by goals
5. Motivator   -   Keeps team moving towards goals
6. Enthusiast   -   Keeps team flowing together
7. Regulator   -   Keeps abreast of all quality measures and monitors all areas.

The most valuable asset is people. Without people nothing around us would be in place. The intangible asset that we tend to dispense with is more valuable than any of the buildings ever built.

Treat your team like the valuable asset they are and you will receive the greatest return.

My Action Points

1. What kind of leader are you?
   (Tick the ones that describe you, be honest)

   Autocratic ...
   Democratic ...
   Transactional ....
   Enabling ......
   Controlling .....
   Charismatic ....
   Non – Charismatic ....

2. What qualities do you express?

3. What qualities does your team see?

4. Identify your C.A.S.H

    Coach...................................

    Analyst..................................

    Solicitor................................

    Helpers................................

9 Create Your Message

> I have a dream, that my four little children will one day live in a nation where they will not be judged by the color of their skin but by the content of their character. I have a dream today.
> (Martin Luther King, Jr.,)

Martin Luther King became famous for one speech that became the central theme to the struggles that he was fighting in America in the 1960's.

"I Have A Dream"

"I Have A Dream", his speeches came back to this central theme, challenging America to dream again and fight for the equal rights of all its citizens. He was not campaigning for a political post because he was not a politician. He connected with the hearts and minds of people struggling to live and fighting for justice.

Every person brings a gift, the ability to learn and a talent to this earth. No one comes empty handed. You may feel so at

Every person brings a gift

times when things are not going to plan. The key is discovering what you have brought and sharing it with the rest of us. You will need help to unwrap and develop whatever that gift is, using other peoples' experiences.

There is an art or skill in transmitting or communicating your ideas and concept so that 80% of the people understand what you are saying 20% of the time.

The purpose of communicating your message is to educate, entertain and inspire others to take action and change their lives with your products or services.

Telling Stories have Always Been a Powerful Form of Communicating

Telling stories have always been a powerful form of communicating a given culture, set of values and custom from one generation to the next. Pre-modern times saw families spending time together sharing their stories of adventure and curiosity.

In the magic of metaphor it states that throughout the history of mankind stories have played a part in learning at all levels, from the everyday to the sacred, closing the gap between our individual experience as human beings and the theories we create to explain our experience.

Stories convey a message

Stories help to paint a picture that immediately conveys a message once the story is heard. All around us we see history that has been passed on through stories.

His or Her – Story forms the basis of our history today throughout the world, regardless of race or location. It is the one thing that can bring people together to share for a moment.

Most people believe their story does not matter, or is of little value to anyone.

But people want to hear stories of success, overcoming battles, overcoming illnesses, facing the challenges of life to give them the motivation to continue with their own lives.

What can stories do for us?

1. Give us hope for the future.
2. Restore our faith.
3. Communicate effectively.
4. Bring people together.
5. Put a smile on our face.
6. Teach a point.
7. Reframe the world.
8. Solve a problem.

Your story is a personal testimony of what you have either heard or seen or experienced. It provides a frame in which you can think or justify your behaviour. It provides an opportunity for you to speak and no one can challenge it because it is just a story.

In addition to having a story there is an art in telling that story so everyone wants to listen to connect with your world and live the experience for a short moment. That is a great oratory skill that you can develop and must, in order to communicate more effectively.

Art in telling your story

Building a Pipeline

Once upon a time there were two guys Alan and Donald, ambitious and intelligent both looking for an opportunity in their lives. They lived in a far away village where people had to fetch water in buckets on a daily basis. The chief of the village decided to pay for water to be delivered to the village and invited all the able young men to apply. Alan and Donald won the contract. Alan was over the moon as the job paid a penny a bucket so he could earn one dollar a day. Alan calculated that at the end of the month he would be able to buy a TV and have money in his pocket.

The first day came and Alan and Donald started carrying the buckets of water to the village. Alan was proud and dreamt of the money. Donald already felt the toil on his arms and shoulders and thought there must be a better way to earn the money.

"Alan, there must be a better way to earn money than carrying buckets of water", said Donald. Alan laughed, "What, this is great I 'm earning". After the first month Alan was excited and started drinking in the local bar buying everyone a drink while Donald was thinking.

"Alan, I have an idea why don't we build a pipeline to transport the water to the village", said Donald. "Who has ever heard of a pipeline in these parts", said Alan. Donald thought about his idea and started digging his pipeline.

Days passed and every evening after carrying buckets of water Donald returned to digging his pipeline. His arms ached but he kept dreaming of this pipeline that would change his life forever. After three months of hard work Alan started to feel the toil and drank to relieve the pain.

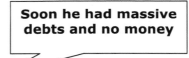

Soon he had massive debts and no money

Soon he had massive debts and no money, his friends deserted him and he sat alone in the bar drinking the pain away.

Donald's pipeline was half done when he said to Alan, "this is a brilliant investment, come and help me so we can finish this". After months of hard work and pain Alan began to see what Donald was saying and helped him complete the pipeline.

The villagers were excited they now had a pipeline bringing water to the village. Donald became a local celebrity and earned money from everyone who connected to the pipeline. When Donald saw how profitable this was he started to invite other young men to join him and build pipelines all over the world. With all the lessons he had learnt he could do this in less than two years.

Most made excuses saying they had no time, they had seen it before and it does not work. (Paraphrased from the pipeline).

What is the moral of this story, building pipelines verses carrying buckets? What is the central message?

What is your mission?

Before you can communicate your message, we must consider "What is your message?" but this can only be understood in the context of why you are here. What do you consider your purpose to be in life?

Mission is defined as a duty or a group sent abroad for specific work. It is a specific task that you were sent to earth to do, carry out or make happen. It determines your life contribution when you become fully connected with your mission. But most people are unsure as to why they are here. They have not spent enough time considering the WHY?

So how do we describe what you are about? What words sum up what you like doing? Review and answer the following questions.

1) What value do you add?

2) How do you make people feel?

3) What action do people take after?

4) How do you see yourself?

5) What gets you excited?

6) What do you see as a big problem?

7) What solutions do you think about?

Please re-read your answers and reflect on what you have written.

Now ask the people closest to you the same question and make a note of their answers. Please do not question their response.

My Action Points

1. How does this exercise make you feel?

2. Are there any points on which you disagree?

3. List five key themes from this exercise.

4. Using the themes create five sentences that explain what you would do in each case.

10 Build Your Stage

God does not judge us by the multitude of works we perform,
but how well we do the work that is ours to do.
(Dr Dale E. Turner)

Every day you wake up and dress for the stage where you perform. That performance determines the life you live, but how prepared are you for that stage? Michael Jackson was one of the greatest performers of our generation, always prepared. A polished performance does not happen overnight, it takes practice.

The Performer

I am sure you are not going to try and imitate Michael Jackson but think about it, every move you make, every decision you take, is being interpreted by someone. It could be your boss, a potential client or customer, a headhunter wanting to recruit you. If that is the case then you must be ready at all times to perform.

There are six keys you must be aware of:

1) Know your art
2) Overcome your fear
3) Connect with people
4) Market your genius
5) Perform your art
6) Be passionate
7) Understand the business

Know Your Art

Artists like Michael Jackson practised so well until they mastered their art. Achieving mastery in any sport or activity is a lengthy process of training and development.
The discipline of training at set times, learning the rules or routines until it becomes a part of you. Mohammed Ali has been deemed the greatest boxer despite retiring from the ring over thirty years ago.

You can only reach mastery if you love what you are doing so much that if you did not get paid you would still do it.

Overcome the Fear

Achieving mastery requires you to face your fears and do it anyway, despite the doubts. Negative self-talk is very powerful when you least expect it. The biggest moment of your life and suddenly you cannot perform. Whenever something new is attempted fear and doubt appear like two brothers unable to leave you, trying to beat you into submission. When Susan Boyle stepped onto the stage of Britain's Got Talent to perform for the first time, I wonder how she felt?

Connecting with people

Some comedians connect quite easily with the audience while performing, much better than politicians, I wonder why? The audience hanging on to every word wanting more. What creates the magnet attraction?

Churchill was known for his leadership of the United Kingdom during World War 11 with his speeches and radio broadcasts, refusing to accept defeat or compromise helped inspire British resistance against the Germans.

Any market researcher will tell you that you must take time to know your audience, their likes and dislikes. Learn their behaviour patterns so you can tap into it. Supermarket and advertising agencies have mastered this technique very well. Creating adverts that compel you to shop and positioning products in the store where you are most likely to buy.

The ability to build a quick rapport with the audience is also very important to gain their trust. One of my speech experts, Craig Valentine, suggests that you must never speak about yourself "I" to your audience. Remain "you" focused, so that in the midst of one hundred customers, there is a feeling of you talking directly to them.

Market Your Genius

What is the point of being very good at something and no one knows. Raising awareness of your particular skill is necessary. We live in a market driven society where things are changing all the time and you may become unemployed. So what skills do you have? How are you developing them? You may have a solution for which someone is prepared to pay a large sum.

Perform Your Art

You must perform regularly or as the saying goes practise makes perfect. Every area of life has people who have spent a lot of years performing, like dancers, singers, actors and practitioners of most disciplines. Where the difficulty arises is where there is a change in career or a new skill being developed. The time-frame required to learn the new skill can be very long. But with time all the new moves can be learned. Over the years I have realised that the best way of learning is to find someone to teach, find a student and stay two steps ahead. This worked well for teaching Sunday School at Church.

Understand the business

Every activity that exchanges money for that activity has a monetary value. Deciding what the value is or how much can be charged is sometimes very difficult. The ability to sell that product or service, present your idea to a group of possible investors and close the sale is vital to running the business. So what do you really need to run any business?

1. Ability to sell and close sales
2. Ability to get new customers
3. Ability to retain customers
4. Ability to price your products
5. Ability to make a profit
6. Ability to collect the money, cash is king.
7. Understand the contracts
8. Plan ahead
9. Make decisions
10. Manage the operations
11. Employ the right people
12. Maintain the records
13. Build relationships
14. Cast the Vision

This works for any business whether a sole trader or solopreneur, mumpreneur, a private company or Plc listed on the stock exchange.

It is your responsibility to be the best at what you do so everyone can see your value.

11 Redefine Your Success

We are successful when we achieve
objectives we have established in advance.
(Tony Jeary)

A definition of success, which I have read over and over again, is that of Jim Rohn, Success is the progressive achievement of goals that have been set in advance. So anyone can be a success providing that they are moving closer to goals they have set.

The majority of people live their lives influenced by their parents, friends, teachers and significant others. Consequently  there is no clear path to where they want to go. It has not been settled in their minds, within themselves, a clear mental picture. The goals you have settled on tend to reflect the people who have influenced you the most, in the time you have been on earth.

Are you settling where you are?

Success is one of those subjects that is never really settled but changes, as you get older.

The clarity of the earlier years get dim, they darken. You become less optimistic and hopeful then settle where you are.

What is Success?

Success is about determining what you want to do with the time you have left. It is anything that you decide and purpose in your mind.

What is Your Gold Standard

Years ago we used to have a gold standard where the banks had to keep a sum of gold in reserves. There was a minimum requirement that was set and all the major banks had to comply.

What are the minimum requirements you have set for your life, your gold standard?

Notice I did not mention silver or even bronze, why? We are all entitled to the best in life, the best food, clothes, home and education, so set your personal gold standard.

There is a gap between what you are entitled to as a human being and what you obtain, it is called the achievement gap. You only achieve what you work for.

Setting Sail

Think about the wind, can a sailor change the force of the wind or the direction? No, the force of nature is far more powerful, but he can use the force to get to where he wants to. As long as he sets the sail in the direction he wants to go and wait for the right wind.

The wind of opportunity that blows may never return to you, you must be ready. In reality you do not just sit and wait for things to happen. You are always in a state of preparing.

Success is your destination but you have to find the wind of opportunity that will assist you in getting there. But in any journey there will be a number of sites you want to see, stops to make and meal breaks. They are all part of your Success MAP.

Success Map

Success maps consist of the goals you have set for yourself to keep on track. Goal setting is the sail we were speaking about earlier. I also like to think of the  good news you bring when you discuss your dreams. It becomes your personal gospel.

What is this gospel?

It is the good news that will change your life when you discover the path to follow. Think in terms of what it stands for:

G Goals
O Objectives
S Strategy
P Plan
E Excitement
L Leadership

1) What goals have you set for yourself for this year, January to December? Make a list.

    a. What do you have to do each month to achieve them?

    b. There are four weeks in a month, what are you doing each week?

    c. There are five working days in a week, what are your daily targets?

      d. There are twenty our hours in a day, what are you doing?

2) What are your objectives?

3) What is the strategy, how?

4) What is the plan?

5) Are you excited? How are you planning to maintain this enthusiasm?

6) Have you found a coach or a mentor?

7) What leadership skills do you require?

      a. What do you have to do each month to achieve them?

      b. There are four weeks in a month, what are you doing each week?

      c. There are five working days in a week, what are your daily targets?

Each of the points above represent a milestone in your journey to achieve that dream or Big Holy Audacious Goals.

The Fastest Route Leads to........

We share a definition of success which is based on the fastest route to get the toys that adults play with.

In this chase we sometimes forget who is in our path, that is not our concern just get me the new game, new TV, new car or house, we need the latest model.

Who says this is the way it should be?

What if we sought to serve first, before our latest needs are met? Creating a culture to serve each other. Showing greater respect for the elderly and the weaker sections of our community.

That means not just based on the ability to pay but take care of those who need it most and who served us diligently in past years so that we can have the lives we now do.

How would that impact the society in which we live?

Would that change the mindset of a young generation who are only interested in what's in it for them?

What kind of world would you like to see?

What would you do to make that a reality?

Your Road Map

How do you rate in all these areas, 1-5 or 6–10. 1 being the lowest and 10 being the highest you can achieve.

- You have a burning desire to do or make something happen knowing what you really want.

- You are facing the reality of your situation realising that the road is filled with obstacles or hurdles.

- You are being enthusiastic every day.

- You have changed your attitude realising it is your greatest asset.

- You know you were born to work so you are now doing the work you love.

- You are focusing on your goals to bring the results you desire.

- You are building a team to assist you.

- You have created your message to the world so there is no confusion.

- You are building your stage to interface with the public, a part-time business, a home business.

- You realise success is not guaranteed and have developed a road map of your goals, understanding your personal gospel.

Visionaries make things happen, they see from afar and then take massive action to accomplish their dreams. If the total of your scores is below 60 then you need further assistance.

My Action Points

Complete this statement.

My dream is to ....

....

Which I will accomplish in ....

It will help me to ....

I am designed for ....but it matters

how I get there because I have the seeds of ....

within me.

12 Your Legacy

Bob Safford speaks of an artistic gene that runs in his family, and there is definitely something artistic about the way he has created his life. The early brush strokes began when - as a child growing up on the "wrong side of the tracks" in Buffalo, New York - he was given a lot of freedom and love but little else. He spent his early days dreaming of something bigger and had the intelligence, imagination, and energy to make it happen.
(The Bob Safford Legacy)

The term legacy means a gift of will of money or other personal property. Something transmitted by or received from an ancestor or predecessor.

The practical application is to make sure you leave an inheritance for your children and their children. So an insurance policy of some kind would probably do the job.

My perception changed in 2011 when I sat in a seminar listening to the late Bob Safford Senior share his 76 years of wisdom of achieving success in his life.

> **His achievements were not just for himself**

He explained that his achievements were not just for himself but along the way it has allowed him the privilege of serving thousands of people. He considered it an honour and a privilege.

Bob Safford had seen hard times being a child of the 1930's depression but had risen above his challenges to become a millionaire. At 22 he had asked a mentor how to become a millionaire.

To become a millionaire find an expert and do what they tell you

He was told to find an expert and do exactly what they told him to do.

He spoke passionately about having a clear concise mental picture of what you want to achieve.

At 76 he was funny, alert and had so much wisdom to share. The audience could not get enough. Sadly a few months later he passed away.

I realised there and then that is what I want to become, a man who has a passion for people, leaving a trail dedicated to helping others while achieving his dream.

I wrote my last chapter one chapter ago, Redefining Success finishing on a high but I realised that the greatest accomplishment is to achieve your dreams and leave a legacy.

That is the reason for this last chapter in memory of a great man Bob Safford Senior to encourage the millions of people that will be reading this book to think carefully about what they will be leaving behind, Your Legacy.

It is not enough to leave a physical estate for the next generation, money can disappear overnight and I have seen it happen to families.

I believe we must create a lot more than money to leave to the next set of families, parents, leaders and politicians because that is what our children are becoming. Here is my list, you can add more as appropriate.

- A belief system
- A clear set of values
- A dream to aspire to
- A plan to help them achieve
- A caring spirit to help others
- A sense of family
- A balanced way of thinking

What are you creating to leave as your legacy? How will the people who have crossed your path remember you?

These are the things we rarely think about.

One thing is clear we never know when our time will expire...

I know you are probably saying I have plenty of time left; I am not ready to go. One thing is clear we never know when our time will expire we just have to be prepared.

Steven Covey in his book the Seven Habits of Highly Effective People, says to imagine your final day at your funeral service. What would you like them to say about you?

My Action Points

Make a decision today how you would like to be remembered.

Think about your family, friends, relationships and all the groups you participate in.

Now what actions do you have to take?

I Will Succeed

I will Succeed because I have a Dream

I will Succeed because I am facing my Reality

I will Succeed because I am Enthusiastic about life

I will Succeed because I have a million pound asset, a changed Attitude

I will Succeed because I have a Message

I will Succeed because I have redefined my Success

Why will you Succeed?

No more excuses - Sotonye Diri

The Work We Were Born to Do – Nick Williams

Rich Dad Poor Dad – Robert T. Kiyosaki

Brand You – John Purkiss & David Royston-Lee

Speak and Grow Rich - Dottie Walters, Lilly Walters

Design Your Best Year Ever - Darren Hardy

The Safford Legacy – Primerica

Goals - Brian Tracey

Developing New Business Ideas – Mary Bragg and Andrew Bragg

Quotational Quotes

Magic of Metaphor - Nick Owen

Walking with the wise -Linda Forsythe

Speak to win - Brian Tracy

Solution Focused Coaching - Jane Greene and Anthony H Grant

Developing the Leader Within You - John C Maxwell

Strategic Acceleration - Tony Cleary

How to Get from Where You are to Where you Want to Be - Jack Cranfield

How They Made A Million (The Dyke and Dryden story) – Tony Wade